NOKADDISH
Poems in the Void

Hanoch Guy-Kaner

Ben Yehuda Press
Teaneck, New Jersey

NOKADDISH: POEMS IN THE VOID ©2020 Hanoch Guy-Kaner. All rights reserved.
No part of this book may be used or reproduced in any manner whatsoever without written permission except in the case of brief quotations embodied in critical articles and reviews.

Published by Ben Yehuda Press
122 Ayers Court #1B
Teaneck, NJ 07666

http://www.BenYehudaPress.com

To subscribe to our monthly book club and support independent Jewish publishing, visit https://www.patreon.com/BenYehudaPress

Jewish Poetry Project #12   **http://jpoetry.us**

Ben Yehuda Press books may be purchased at a discount by synagogues, book clubs, and other institutions buying in bulk. For information, please email markets@BenYehudaPress.com

ISBN13 978-1-934730-86-7

20 21 22 / 10 9 8 7 6 5 4 3 2 1   20200428

I humbly follow in the footsteps of:

Jacob Glatshteyn,
Aaron Zeitlin,
Moshe Leyb Halpern,
Raizl Zichlinsky,
H. Leivick,
Uri Zvi Greenberg,
Isaiah Spiegel.

Contents

Shabbat shalom	1
No Innocence	2
Could Not Help It	3
Horseradish	4
Off Monday	5
Night After Passover	7
God's Fair I	8
God's Fair II	9
I AM אָנוֹכִי	10
Short version	12
Favorites	13
Out of the equation	14
At the curb	15
Fatigue	17
Please sign	20
On Shabbat	21
god's Warehouse	22
Blessings	23
god calls me	25
The Second Day	26
Between Me and You	27
Wings	28
Back to the Garden	29
Between the Spaces	30
No Fasting	31
The Gate of Mercy	32
YOU ARE	33
Aleph	34
Bet	35
Gimmel	36
Dalet	37
Heh	38
Vav	39
Zayin	40
Het	41
Thunderstorms	42
Shepherd	43
Ignorant Believers	44
Twelve Gates	45
Paradise Delicious	46

When the Sea Parted	47
Serpent	48
Commandments	49
Because You Have Chosen Us	50
Egypt	51
No dominion	52
Ascent	53
Mount Moses	54
There	55
About the poet	56
Other books by Hanoch Guy Kaner	57

Shabbat shalom

Wrapped in a blue prayer shawl
Gaston prays to Señor God.
in a sweet tenor
he lingers on:
Kadosh   Kadosh   Kadosh
We are only nine in the small chapel
captivated by the ascending prayer
of Spanish and Hebrew
in Gaston's soft voice.
Eyes closed, he chants:
Amen.
Sela.

Addresses us
as an audience of a thousand worshipers
at the Temple in Jerusalem.
Eighty years old, both Judith and Hanna sigh.
A young American tourist wipes away a tear.
Felix Koch's severe face brightens.
Gaston lingers lovingly on the Hebrew.

I am hanging on every word,
the chapel is steeped in light emanations.

Gaston forgets the small chapel in Sosúa Dominicana,
transported safely in his blue prayer shawl
to Mount Carmel's beautiful peak.
His sweet voice rolls down and echoes in the valley,
words melt under his tongue.

He wakes with a start.
Whispers Shabbat shalom.

No Innocence
left
in Adam or Eve or the garden.
The only one who remained
naive was the snake who
thought it was all his doing.
Fig tree looked
on a tormented pale God.
Nothing worse for him than everything
going according to plan.
When night fell heavy
little luminous moons
floated in the garden,
while candles burned
under fig trees
shedding red and white
tear-swords.
A pale God was thrown out of the garden.
The gate slammed behind him,
the angels went in business for themselves.

Could Not Help It

In the beginning the earth was red hot.
Winds rushing madly across the meadows.
Poppy flowers huge and tall sunflowers
surrounded Avram's house.
God was young and impetuous
lusted after Avram,
told him to defy King Nimrod, leave for another desert.
He was determined to have him and made him
outrageous promises such as:
Your descendants will be as many as the stars in heaven,
or more numerous than the grains of sand.
He meant every word but
broke every promise.

Reluctantly he put on a magical fire show.
Felt sorry for his most loyal prophet Moses.
His love affair was doomed
and still he promised, threatened, seduced.

When the Israelites forced Aaron to mold the golden calf,
he danced with them.
In a fury fit Moses broke the first set of tablets.

Horseradish

He is in the dishwasher
having his way with the dishes
in a terrible racket.
God scares the cat,
flies out to the fridge
writing his name in sudsy letters,
knocking down Elijah's cup of wine,
breaking a matzah plate.
Hey, it's your commandments.

Be careful!

He dips a carrot in the horseradish dish.
Sneezes.
The Haggadah falls to the floor.
Slams the door to the patio
where he goes out for a smoke.
Didn't you hear, smoking is bad for you?
Mind your own Jewish business.
He snaps
Finish the Seder.

Off Monday

God took off the Monday of
the Virginia massacre.

He takes off most days,
not giving an audience even to his most faithful.
Moses and Jesus.
His shrink is certain that it is either
Post-partum from the third creation,
a severely seven-way split personality
or optimal narcissism.
Test results pending.
He has despaired of the tenants downstairs,
promises repairs,
lets the place run down to the ground.

A glimpse of his beloved sends
him into rage.
Reminders of
deranged Cain or
of killers in Madame Tussauds wax museum.

Bored angels
linger in casinos
or whore houses.
Some even join gangs of the Dark One
in Columbia and slums.

He rarely comes into the office.
Papers spill off desks.
SOS voicemail from prophets
go unanswered.
Computer hard drives freeze.
His subjects' personal files
litter his yard and the garden.

God plays golf.
Most of his balls
end up in
swamp.

Night After Passover

God plays
poker
loses big
gets plastered,
relinquishes control of the book of deaths
to the demons and their half-brother devils
with rotten teeth
who happily steal
the red book of suffering.
They follow his notes,
gleefully assign people
to be blessed for the year
to be remembered, forgotten
commit successful suicide,
shoot heroin,
doomed to die from a plague in an Indian cave.

Then for the fun of it,
they mix up the list and make bets.

Little demons having a hilarious time assigning fates
ignoring the archangel notes,
They decide:

Who will be a drug food sex depression addict.
They work in a hurry lest God will wake up
and erase the data base and
install a virus that makes it impossible
to restore people to health.

God wakes up with a hangover and concurs with the demons.

God's Fair I

God gorges on strawberries.
Cannot resist them,
succulent and bright red.
He gives the last one to Sarah,
who gets pregnant.
Fruit seekers are turned away
by embarrassed angels.
God grabs two strawberries at a time
and gets them all over
his white robe.
No strawberries for Adam and Eve.
Let them grow their own
outside the garden.

God's Fair II

On the first day after creation,
God took off his yarmulke
and put on his t-shirt
emblazed with fluorescent
       I
Adam stood at the gate collecting donations.
Gabriel blew huge bubbles while Raphael
invited all to his healing tent.
Uriel shot comets through the seven skies.
And little Angels sprayed the guests with huge water guns.
Frostiel distributed rainbow sherbet.
A 2k race was announced,
and God came last, red faced and out of breath.
He collapsed in a lawn chair
and ordered a Jerusalem martini from Methuselah.
Clean up the mess, old fart.
Recycle the glass and plastic.
And lock up the place
until next year.

I AM אָנוֹכִי

At midnight God closes all
windows and doors.
Puts on Satan's alarm,
skips one window to
allow in an urgent messenger
escaping the night dogs ready to
tear him apart in the devil's open pit.

God tucks the angels
in cloud beds.
Forbids them to sing praises, blessings 'till dawn.
Secures the roses around the house.
Checks for leaks in the sky dome
that could flood the earth.
Locks the sun in the barn.
Lets the moon out of the attic.
Shakes stars out from his sleeves
Sleeps fitfully.

Bands of hooded militia crows dump souls screeching
the dome windows and doors shake violently.
Another rebellion
of priests on Mount Moriah
wakes him up.
Wrapped souls
ready for delivery
unravel,
shoot down rapidly
cry out.
An angel has a nightmare.
Stars are consumed by dragon holes.
A black paw hides the moon.
Dawn descends.

Hanoch Guy-Kaner

The angels' soft hymns
give him a splitting headache.
Forgets to let the sun out,
Tuck the moon in a straw bed in the attic.

Time to open the windows and doors
to the usual parade of hagglers, supplicants, false prophets
and spiritual impersonators.

Short version

I am donot donot donot donot donot donot donot
(honorremember)

Favorites

It is all about him.
god does not have favorites.
Just step-sons and daughters
standing in line for a handout.
Lucky, they don't have to deal
with a stepmother he divorced
millennia ago.

Out of the equation

Take god out of the equation.
Create a space
in which man and woman
look at each other with wonder.
Take out of the equation
the wonder of man and woman,
the vast desert remains
weeping for rain.
Desert disappears.
The equation is sucked
into sinkholes.
by the dead sea.

Giant dogs
spit sand
filling the rivers.

I have been through
steel and wooden crosses,
through priests,

fake rabbis with yellowing teeth,
veiled crescents and masked Bedouins.
I've been through fury and mercy,
through gods more silent than idols.

I was sprinkled by sacred water
Waded through polluted holy rivers.

I've left rusting gods
in junkyards.
Sit by the road
in a clown suit
throwing mud at
used gods salesmen.

Hanoch Guy-Kaner

At the curb

god sits at the corner of Nevada and Utah
between boarded houses banished by the union of beggars.
His polyester pants have seen better days.
Faded suspenders falling apart.
In the best tradition of hated prophets
he goes hungry most of the time.
Whispers to himself snatches of psalm
Frustrated he cannot remember the end of
"The lord is my...."
Forgot even the first commandment.

Sometimes Joe the wino comes by.
Takes him out to dinner at McDonald's.
He loves their super fries.

He mumbles divine phrases he thundered to
Moses on the Mount.
Forgets most.
He wishes he had the vision of the chariot Ezekiel had
In the back of his mind.
Sodom and Gomorra are lovely.

He drops in churches synagogues.
Bored to tears by the sermons.
Gets hives from the liturgy.
He adopted the habit
of stealing from collection boxes.
Snores in the back,
gets thrown out.

He is fascinated by the intricate calligraphy in mosques.
Taught himself Arabic.
He wanders into museums, seeks the Saints section
Gets furious with them:
They got it all wrong

Where are the lepers cripples stray cats and donkeys?

He is seething with the curse of never getting old.
The angel of Death shuns him.
Disgusted, Satan won't bargain with him.
God falls at the curb as a bundle waiting
to be picked up with the morning collection.

Fatigue

Amichai writes that dust is
God's fatigue in the world.
Fatigue
grinds God
into fine dust.
He forgets how to put himself together,
as he did effortlessly at the second creation.

Disjointed visions
of palm trees, snakes and angels,
Eve's succulent beauty
floats in front of him.
Frightened by the glint of fiery angels' swords
slamming Eden's gate.
If only one incantation, hymn or psalm
came to him.
How did he mix dust with water?
where can he get water?
create giants, mother, son, sky, ocean?

Nothing but the letter Aleph,
which is no help.
A thunder roars:
Thou are from dust and thou shalt return to dust.
Or was is it: *Dust to dust ashes to ashes.*
Who said it? he screams. *It sounds wrong.*
A single bat takes flight into twilight.

He is a chaos of gases
whirling in dizziness and delirium.
When he is about to give up,
the first letter of Genesis emerges:
BAYT. clear and fierce.
But he is already void.

NO

      KA
         DD
            ISH

Praise the dead all the ways you can
                    Magnify their deeds
                              Give them
credit for good
intentions

Absences from
synagogues.

Wrestling with
cancer and other plagues

For insecurities
          Feeble loves

Being born

Do not praise
          Do not bless
                Honor
                      Glorify
                            Exalt
                                god.
Inscribe him in the books of the

Indifferent to

Hanoch Guy-Kaner

Starvation draughts genocide tsunamis Aids ALS global warming and foreclosures

Hug the living
        Bathe them with tenderness
                      Be patient with their bad behavior

                      Help them carry
the load of the dead

                  Surround them with beauty and splendor

For being exquisite in a short life

                  Treasure
them with the present
Cuddle them in warm memories

                  Do not make any demands

Be silent with them

                  Meditate peace for abandoned souls

Please sign

Contract
against all clauses, sub-clauses, stipulations,
conditional blessings,
unconditional penalties.
Delete the Yom Kippur prayer book bulging
with pleas, whining, angst,
eighty varieties of guilt and praises.

Drop any expectation of prayers.
Apologize in writing for your misdeeds,
cruelty, agony destruction you caused us.

Take back all injunctions
No fasting.
No promises.

Your track record proves
your words are worthless.

Your fasts turned into feasts
Your names erased.

Hanoch Guy-Kaner

On Shabbat

I am jealous of Rivka Miriam,
bright forehead,
colorful kerchief,
lips singing faith and thanks.
She builds a special attic for God
small or big,
expands and shrinks
according to the needs.
At twilight they paint the garden,
add fragrances.
Daily she brings up his meal
of dates, figs, and a pomegranate.

She accepts his genocides
celebrates her parents' escape from the Khurbn,
praises Jerusalem,
grateful to live by the walls
in Israel's miracles.

She calls God out of the attic
to the playground.
They dance in the light rain,
swing in the wind
on Mount Olives' cooling evening.

god's Warehouse

They promised me a long shelf life.
I grew accustomed to restricted movement,
the semi-darkness,
angels and loud prayers.
From time to time,
I hear distant children sing
with laughter bells.
I am used to being moved
from shelf to shelf
being dusted off,
wrapped in canvas.

Changes are slow.
I am adapting.
One day, the roof will cave in.

Hanoch Guy-Kaner

Blessings

In the beginning there was cancer, diabetes and asthma
on the face of the earth.
god said to cancer and his mates:
"Rule the earth."

Smoking leisurely his cigar
On Yom Kippur 5764,
he cleared his calendar
and showered special women with gifts.
He awarded Trudy Wright with ovarian cancer
that was not diagnosed until
the freedom feast of Passover.
Bonnie Brown was fortunate to acquire multiple sclerosis.
Two women among the thousands
who experienced the mighty one's ultimate compassion.

Amichai wrote that god is full of compassion.
If he was not full of compassion
there will be some left for the world.

There will be some left for D'vorah, Faye,
and their bald sisters
poisoned by chemotherapy radiation
and counterdrugs.

At the closing prayer of Yom Kippur
Jews were jubilant.
Except Trudy, D'vorah and Faye,
who spend their time in wasp gardens,
with the massacred, butchered and gassed millions
and other recipients of
God's grace, compassion and love,
who are crowded in the yards of the waxing moon

waiting to be shipped to heaven's
concentration camps.

god calls me

I'm not home
I call
He's not home
not even an answering machine
or a little angel
on the night shift

Outside all is in order
Stars are lit
the pale moon sickle
hangs up there and swings
The ocean still roars
Shells are disintegrating on the beach

The Second Day

On the second day of Rosh Hashanah
we came down the path
to pray by the creek.
In the middle of the service
a white horse
galloped through the water
and sprayed us.
Towards the end a wild dog
stole my shoe.
Sophia softened the path
with clear laughter.

Between Me and You

We are separated by holidays
of two days, seven days
and eight days.
Between us
long hours in the synagogue,
dense pages of an endless liturgy of hymns,
medieval prayers and poems,
and numerous Kaddish for the dead.

I hope to be able to sit on the deck
on a regular day without prayer interruptions
and have a friendly talk.

Wings

Let us magnify his holiness,
lovingkindness and compassion.
How lovely his tents are.
Beloved Sarah is under the divine wings.
Let her be bound in the garland of lives.
How fortunate is Sarah,
Born on the first day of Passover
Died on the second day of Rosh Hashanah,
When the gates of heaven are wide open as on Yom Kippur.
Angels chant soft hymns,
Ascending and descending ladders of light.

Mourners bathe in compassion, memory,
winter's soft light coming through
stained glass windows.

The more Rabbi Linda piles up thanks to god,
recites his compassion and kindness,
The harder I am smothered by wings,
Crushed by the closing gate.

Back to the Garden

sucking on red succulent strawberries
devouring sticky dates
drinking coconut milk

cracking nuts one by one
enjoying yellow, red and white candle lights

White juices turn red
in a magical switch.

I was present
and God hides
behind a tree
whispers:
You are my Gentle keeper,
Rename the fruits

Between the Spaces

So much god in me.
I'm mostly air, space and water
and the Shekhinah
is hovering above the water
and traveling
through the spaces
illuminated
god is nesting in my spaces
and I'm in his.
The partnership is solid
made out of spaces.

No Fasting

Where those who fast
I do not stand.
I am where the wind moves gently.
The woods are dense
and the slope is steep.
I climb the path,
look at the golden wheat fields
and the does roaming.
If I can't write,
I sit quietly by the electric fence,
look at the reflection of an old house in the creek.
My throat burns.
Memories of Jerusalem erased.

I am going where
the wind moves gently.

The Gate of Mercy

At the end of Yom Kippur,
honey cake and wine consumed.
The angel of mercy left the gate slightly open,
so the dead will have a chance
to escape.
He even lights a full moon
to show them the way.
But the dead
who were almost pardoned
cling to the fence,
refuse the offer to go back.

They'd rather stay.
Memory lightening
terrifies them.
Son murdered.
Families
torn apart.

Drowning lovers
scorch their skulls.
They'd rather suffer
at heaven's gates,
force their soul to forget the living.
and mercy-heavy, the gate
remains open.

Hanoch Guy-Kaner

YOU ARE

Aleph

You are
The uncertainty of my next breath
the tremors in my capillaries
the caresses of inner starved skin
tickling my baby feet
tugging of my beard by my unborn grandson
The fluttering of lung leaves
seduction of the long tentacles of a giant electric squid
in the ocean's depth
luminous crowns on top of the dancing waves
in the Mediterranean Sea.
You are trembling with pups of an ice seal
deep below the snow
in the eye of the sand storm which
hurls me like a thorny bush
from sand dune to sand dune
the gentle hand that turns me towards
Jerusalem

.

Bet

You are the union of
African volcanoes and Alaskan glaciers
The Grand Canyon and the tiny Ramon canyon in
southern Israel.

Black flies that crown the rhinoceros.
You are the troubled genius and sweet Down's syndrome
twins
the cripple who struggles to cross the street
and the cancer survivor biker who completes a 75 km race.
You are the boy who spits and whistles in synagogue on
Yom Kippur
and the forgiving rabbi.

You despise the pious fasting and just preach.
Guide those who spend their days with the hospice
patients.
You enjoy harboring frightened dwarfs under moonlit
mushrooms,
crush termites' towers and scatter them east of Eden.

Gimmel

You are the feeble god
You need help
crossing the street.
My shortness of breath
and the urgency to urinate,
You are the war criminal and the abused child.
You do not forgive martyrs
and overlook sins.

You are hard on yourself
and soft on rebels

Dalet

You are
the peace of
finger to finger
hair to hair
red blood cells
to white blood cells.
Bubbles of oxygen to
bubbles of carbon monoxide.
Cheery goodbyes and
teary farewells.
Fast exchanges
of fluids.

Hymns of awe
flowing sweetly
scattering low notes and chants
through veins and arteries
bone marrow and lymph springs
and my age spots.

Heh

Among the faces of God
above the waters is a wrinkled
toothless wise woman.
Among the faces is a mean looking
giant who puts a fist in my face
a delicate spider web
swaying in the wind.

Among your others are

shamans and painted tribal chiefs.
Among the hands is a sore
on my thumb
Among your canopies
 a checkered colorful blanket
we bought on our wedding day

Vav

Honey light rivers flow between palm trees
surrounded by golden reeds.
Tall banana trees and fragrant pomegranates.
Deserts replaced suddenly by silver palaces and marble castles.
Ancient olive groves cover Galilee mountains.
Vineyards bursting with purple Muscat grapes.

The divine carries twigs, leaves and acacia yellow balls,
builds cozy nests in the crevices
and caves of Mount Carmel humming lullabies.
He is watching light streaks dive into the Mediterranean
and falls asleep in his nests covered with dew and pine needles.

Zayin

What does God think about
so many quiet Chinese
two billion Indians
and so few loud Jews
and the angels
who are sentenced to sing praises
doomed to be suspended
between heaven and earth.
Bridges on fire?

Does he lust
after Barbie dolls
with gaudy jewelry?
Where does he file
so many complaints requests,
too much submission
praises and awe?

When she looks
in the great water
what does she see?

Het

For Mitch

God is playing
on 64 trillion screens.
Impossible to get
a composite picture.
I wonder what plays
on every screen,
changes from one second to the other
How do his huge paint brushes move quickly using
gallons upon gallons
of blue paint drums
to draw just a small sky section
with a few clouds

and what he has for
breakfast?

Thunderstorms

Loud thunderstorms
and a blinding lightening.
The children in the synagogue
are happy:
At least god said something.

Shepherd

Who is the shepherd in charge
of multitudes of sheep clouds,
circling airplanes, ships lost in
Bermuda triangles
and mad fires in mountain forests?

Ignorant Believers

Do not seek God's splendor
and fragrance.
Seek not sweetness
and mellow smells and tastes.

He is under pungent mushrooms,
in burnt pita bread,
camel dung and the flies.
His essence is
in a child's blind eye
and in his mother's bloody head wound.

Twelve Gates

Nine gates in Jerusalem walls
between the gate of mercy
and the gate of garbage.
Three gates to heaven.
One for the terrified rich.
Another for pagans,
and at the end of a thorny
neglected path a rusty gate
for the righteous.

Paradise Delicious

The vapors over paradise deliciously dense.
Fruits only to be enjoyed,
not to be named.
Trees fertilize each other.
Fish in the four rivers
speak the same language.
Man sought and not found,
night and day nowhere.
Permanent twilight.
Dry winds met dancing
sea breezes,
grass soared to trees,
fragrant springs flooded the meadows.

Angels stood
in awe.
The gates were wide open,
no man or woman
in or out.

When the Sea Parted

When the sea parted
anemones spread in its midst
purple, white and red.
Palm trees grew
bunches of sweet, fragrant dates.
Every crossing person and child
carried a large pomegranate
on their head.
They walked on a lush carpet of grass
honey dripping from the beehives
in the trees.
On the northern bank
The little bitter lake was its old self
without any trace of the abundance in its belly.

Serpent

Hebrews scared out of their wits bathed by lava.
They gobbled manna mushrooms in the morning.
Whispered they will obey but craved Egyptian steaks.

Moses out of tricks to please them.
The desert opened with vipers, scorpions.
Hebrews scared out of their wits,
Forgot, craved Egyptian steaks.

The desert opened with vipers, scorpions.
Hebrews scared out of their wits.
Whispered they will obey the faith,
Frenzy around the golden calf.

The desert opened with vipers, scorpions.
Moses still in ecstasy on Mount Sinai.

Commandments

We returned them unused.
They were broken.
We have never received them.

Because You Have Chosen Us
after Natan Alterman

Because you have chosen us
with Syrians, Iraqis and Sudanese
to be tortured and massacred
at the foot of your throne.
Because you have not chosen or favored anybody.
Just a few nations
that were plain lucky or forgotten by
monsters and evil ones.
Not chosen.
Not favored.
by you
the indifferent
or missing

Hanoch Guy-Kaner

Egypt

Jews are not the universe's light.
A few escaped through chimneys,
spit out of cattle cars.
Chain severed,
rusted links,
desperately entangled in forest saplings.
Refugees
converted into agnostics.
Their only hope is to go back to Egypt.

No dominion

Contrary to Genesis
you have no dominion over the fishes, birds
or the earth which erupts as it pleases,
whips the plains with tornadoes,
lets the sea unleash tsunamis.
You have no say about
the growing scar in your right eye,
The twitches of your hand,
Your broken vertebra.
Deer in your yard ignore your warning
as do geese who shit over your lawn.
So do raccoons partying at night.

This time Kabir is wrong.
That from one drop a universe emerges.
Better listen to rabbi Akvia:

"You came from a putrid drop."
When you open your front door
You'll be snatched by hooded Satan.

Ascent

Treacherous path up the dense wood.
A hairy fist pushes you up the steepest one.
You stumble through thorny bushes and nettle patches.
Hold on to slippery roots.

You refuse to make the climb.

Tree canopies torn sky pieces swirl.

Legs swollen, bleeding arms, neck punctured by black flies.
Collapse on to a bald boulder.
Trembling knees go on
happen upon a bright clearing.
Drop to your knees.
This is the place.
No house will be built here no tent pitched.
A pine lit by lightening.
Sink deep into a glowing bed of needles.

Your pillow black marble reflecting the dying sun.

Mount Moses

At the wall of the Santa Katarina Monastery in Sinai
soaked in dew by a palm tree
Sweet rabbaba strings at 4 a.m.
shaking the sleeping bag
wary of scorpions
almost stepping on camel dung

A winding path up
little rocks flying
belabored breathing
a shove sends me skidding
a menacing sharp rock pushes me back
a jackal wailing in the shadows
clouds torn.

Dawn opens the peak with white light streaks
Through fog
Monk cells at the edge
and I dance

at the top of Mount Moses
drinking dawn
granite peaks spinning
wings all around
and I dance

There

I knew grace
Like no other.
A tender angel stroked
My forehead.
Another kissed my eyes.
A third
Dripped a honey light
Necklace
In my mouth.

About the poet

Hanoch Guy, Ph.D, Ed.D, spent his childhood and youth in Israel. He is a bilingual poet in Hebrew and English.

Dr. Guy is an emeritus professor of Jewish and Hebrew literature at Temple University. He has taught poetry and mentoring at the Musehouse Center.

He has published his poetry in the U.S, England, Wales, Greece, and Israel.

He won awards from Poetica, Mad Poets Society, Poetry Super Highway, and Philadelphia Poets.

Dr. Guy is the author of seven English poetry collections and a Hebrew poetry collection.

Website: hanochguy-kaner.com

Other books by Hanoch Guy Kaner

The road to Timbuktu: travel poems.

Terra Treblinka: Poems of the Holocaust

We pass each other on the stairs:120 imaginary and real encounters.

Sirocco and scorpions: poems of Israel and Palestine

A green cow (Hebrew)

Springtime in Moldova (2019)

The Jewish Poetry Project

Ben Yehuda Press

From the Coffee House of Jewish Dreamers: Poems of Wonder and Wandering and the Weekly Torah Portion by Isidore Century

"Isidore Century is a wonderful poet. His poems are funny, deeply observed, without pretension." – *The Jewish Week*

The House at the Center of the World: Poetic Midrash on Sacred Space by Abe Mezrich

"Direct and accessible, Mezrich's midrashic poems often tease profound meaning out of his chosen Torah texts. These poems remind us that our Creator is forgiving, that the spiritual and physical can inform one another, and that the supernatural can be carried into the everyday."
—Yehoshua November, author of *God's Optimism*

we who desire: Poems and Torah riffs by Sue Swartz

"Sue Swartz does magnificent acrobatics with the Torah. She takes the English that's become staid and boring, and adds something that's new and strange and exciting. These are poems that leave a taste in your mouth, and you walk away from them thinking, what did I just read? Oh, yeah. It's the Bible."
—Matthue Roth, author, *Yom Kippur A Go-Go*

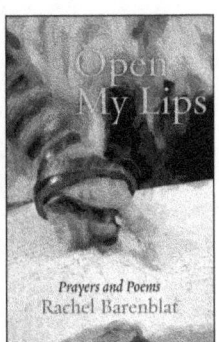

Open My Lips: Prayers and Poems
by Rachel Barenblat

"Barenblat's God is a personal God—one who lets her cry on His shoulder, and who rocks her like a colicky baby. These poems bridge the gap between the ineffable and the human. This collection will bring comfort to those with a religion of their own, as well as those seeking a relationship with some kind of higher power."
—Satya Robyn, author, *The Most Beautiful Thing*

Words for Blessing the World: Poems in Hebrew and English by Herbert J. Levine

"These writings express a profoundly earth-based theology in a language that is clear and comprehensible. These are works to study and learn from."
—Rodger Kamenetz, author, *The Jew in the Lotus*

Shiva Moon: Poems by Maxine Silverman

"The poems, deeply felt, are spare, spoken in a quiet but compelling voice, as if we were listening in to her inner life. This book is a precious record of the transformation saying Kaddish can bring. It deserves to be read. These are works to study and learn from."
—Howard Schwartz, author, *The Library of Dreams*

is: heretical Jewish blessings and poems by Yaakov Moshe (Jay Michaelson)

"Finally, Torah that speaks to and through the lives we are actually living: expanding the tent of holiness to embrace what has been cast out, elevating what has been kept down, advancing what has been held back, reveling in questions, revealing contradictions."
—Eden Pearlstein, aka eprhyme

Texts to the Holy: Poems
by Rachel Barenblat

"These poems are remarkable, radiating a love of God that is full bodied, innocent, raw, pulsating, hot, drunk. I can hardly fathom their faith but am grateful for the vistas they open. I will sit with them, and invite you to do the same."
—Merle Feld, author of A Spiritual Life.

The Sabbath Bee: Love Songs to Shabbat
by Wilhelmina Gottschalk

"Torah, say our sages, has seventy faces. As these prose poems reveal, so too does Shabbat. Here we meet Shabbat as familiar housemate, as the child whose presence transforms a family, as a spreading tree, as an annoying friend who insists on being celebrated, as a woman, as a man, as a bee, as the ocean."
—Rachel Barenblat, author, The Velveteen Rabbi's Haggadah

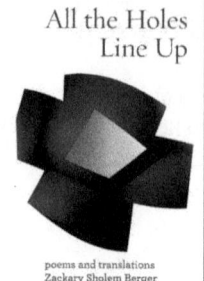

All the Holes Line Up: Poems and Translations
by Zackary Sholem Berger

"Spare and precise, Berger's poems gaze unflinchingly at—but also celebrate—human imperfection in its many forms. And what a delight that Berger also includes in this collection a handful of his resonant translations of some of the great Yiddish poets." —Yehoshua November, author of God's Optimism and Two World Exist

How to Bless the New Moon: The Priestess Paths Cycle and Other Poems for Queens
by Rachel Kann

"To read Rachel Kann's poems is to be confronted with the possibility that you, too, are prophet and beloved, touched by forces far beyond your mundane knowing. So, dear reader, enter into the 'perfumed forcefield' of these words—they are healing and transformative."
—Rabbi Jill Hammer, co-author of The Hebrew Priestess

Into My Garden: Prayers
by David Caplan

"The beauty of Caplan's book is that it is not polemical. It does not set out to win an argument or ask you whether you've put your tefillin on today. These gentle poems invite the reader into one person's profound, ambiguous religious experience."
—The Jewish Review of Books

Between the Mountain and the Land is the Lesson: Poetic Midrash on Sacred Community
by Abe Mezrich

"Abe Mezrich cuts straight back to the roots of the Midrashic tradition, sermonizing as a poet, rather than idealogue. Best of all, Abe knows how to ask questions and avoid the obvious answers."
—Jake Marmer, author, *Jazz Talmud*

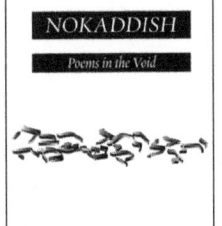

NOKADDISH: Poems in the Void
by Hanoch Guy Kaner

"A subversive, midrashic play with meanings—specifically Jewish meanings, and then the reversal and negation of these meanings."
—Robert G. Margolis

The Jewish Poetry Project
jpoetry.us

www.ingramcontent.com/pod-product-compliance
Lightning Source LLC
LaVergne TN
LVHW041346080426
835512LV00006B/644